The Political Economy of
World Mass Migration

THE HENRY WENDT LECTURE SERIES

The Henry Wendt Lecture is delivered annually at the American Enterprise Institute by a scholar who has made major contributions to our understanding of the modern phenomenon of globalization and its consequences for social welfare, government policy, and the expansion of liberal political institutions. The lecture series is part of AEI's Wendt Program in Global Political Economy, established through the generosity of the SmithKline Beecham pharmaceutical company (now GlaxoSmithKline) and Mr. Henry Wendt, former chairman and chief executive officer of SmithKline Beecham and trustee emeritus of AEI.

GROWTH AND INTERACTION IN THE WORLD ECONOMY:
THE ROOTS OF MODERNITY
Angus Maddison, 2001

IN DEFENSE OF EMPIRES
Deepak Lal, 2002

THE POLITICAL ECONOMY OF WORLD MASS MIGRATION:
COMPARING TWO GLOBAL CENTURIES
Jeffrey G. Williamson, 2004

The Political Economy of
World Mass Migration

Comparing Two Global Centuries

Jeffrey G. Williamson

The AEI Press

Publisher for the American Enterprise Institute

WASHINGTON, D.C.

Available in the United States from the AEI Press, c/o Client Distribution Services, 193 Edwards Drive, Jackson, TN 38301. To order, call toll free: 1-800-343-4499.

Library of Congress Cataloging-in-Publication Data

Williamson, Jeffrey G.

  The political economy of world mass migration / Jeffrey G. Williamson.
      p. cm.
  Includes bibliographical references and index.
    ISBN 0-8447-7181-3 (alk. paper)
    1. Alien labor—Economic aspects. 2. Emigration and immigration—Government policy. 3. Globalization. I. Title.

  HD6300.W55 2004
  331.6'2--dc22
                                                    2004019234

10 09 08 07 06 05 04   1 2 3 4 5

Contents

Illustrations

Acknowledgments

This lecture draws heavily on recent collaborative work with Timothy J. Hatton, especially on our joint forthcoming book, *World Mass Migration: Two Centuries of Policy and Performance*. I also acknowledge with pleasure financial support from the National Science Foundation SES-0001362, and the work environment at the University of Wisconsin Economics Department, where this was written while I was on leave from Harvard.

The Political Economy of
World Mass Migration

Jeffrey G. Williamson

Immigrants during Two Global Centuries:
Rising Quantity and Falling Quality

The first global century took place between about 1820 and World War I, characterized by falling barriers to trade and to the flows of labor and capital. All three boomed. Since about 1950, the second global century has tried to reintegrate these three markets in the wake of the interwar autarchic retreat. This paper is about the political economy of immigration in both global centuries.

Annual immigration to North America and Oceania rose gradually to the mid-1970s before surging to a million per year in the 1990s. The absolute numbers by then were similar to those reached during the age of mass migration about a century earlier, but they were smaller relative to the destination country populations that had to absorb them. The U.S. annual immigration rate fell from 11.6 immigrants per thousand in the 1900s to 0.4 immigrant per thousand in the 1940s, before rising again to 4 immigrants per thousand in the 1990s. The proportion of the U.S. population born in a foreign land had fallen from a 1910 peak of 15 percent to an all-century low of 4.7 percent in 1970. The postwar immigration boom increased the foreign-born share to more than 8 percent in 1990 and more than 10 percent in 2000. Thus, the United States has come two-thirds of the way back to reclaiming the title "a nation of immigrants" after a

1

half-century retreat. While the immigration *rate* is now only a third that achieved at its peak in the first decade of the twentieth century, the contribution of immigration to population and labor force *growth* is similar, because the rate of natural increase has also declined.

What happened to the United States after World War II also happened worldwide. Table 1 reports trends in the foreign born around the world over the thirty-five years since the mid-1960s. The data are based on country censuses, sources that are likely to be of higher quality than those that report annual immigrant flows, and they deal with unambiguous net permanent moves. The most revealing entries appear in the last three rows of the table. There we see that the foreign-born share in the total population increased by about one third in Oceania between 1965 and 2000 (from 14.4 to 19.1 percent), more than doubled in North America (from 6 to 13 percent), and more than tripled in Europe (from 2.2 to 7.7 percent). North America is defined to exclude emigrating Mexico, so in this case we are talking exclusively about a high-wage immigrant-absorbing region. The same is not true of Europe, since it is defined to include Eastern Europe and the former Soviet Union, two net emigrating regions and, increasingly, a significant source of migrants for the European Union (EU). The foreign-born share in *Western* Europe rose much more dramatically than it did for Europe as a whole.

While the Organisation for Economic Co-operation and Development (OECD) immigration has surged, the labor market quality of these immigrants has declined. For example, U.S. immigrant men earned 4.1 percent *more* than native-born men in 1960, but they earned 16.3 percent *less* in 1990 (Borjas 1999, 1724). Some of this was due to the decline in immigrant educational attainment, but when we control for this effect, the adjusted relative wage still fell by 13.3 percent over these thirty years. Recent immigrants always suffer an earnings disadvantage before they assimilate, and that was even true in 1960. But their initial wage relative to the native born deteriorated by 24 percentage points over those thirty years.

Most of this decline in immigrant "quality" is due to changes in the source-area composition of U.S. immigrants (table 2). The current debate over the impact of shifting immigrant source on the labor

TABLE 1
THE MIGRANT STOCK AROUND THE WORLD, 1965–2000

Year	1965	1975	1985	1990a	1990b	2000
Migrant Stock (millions)						
World	75.2	84.5	105.2	119.8	154.0	174.9
Africa	8.0	11.2	12.5	15.6	16.2	16.3
Asia	31.4	29.7	38.7	43.0	50.0	50.0
Latin America/ Caribbean	5.9	5.9	6.4	7.5	7.1	5.9
North America	12.7	15.0	20.5	23.9	27.6	40.8
Europe	14.7	19.5	23.0	25.1	48.4	56.1
Oceania	2.5	3.3	4.1	4.6	4.8	5.8
Percentage of World Migrant Stock						
World	100.0	100.0	100.0	100.0	100.0	100.0
Africa	10.6	13.2	11.9	13.1	10.5	9.3
Asia	41.8	35.1	36.8	35.9	32.4	28.6
Latin America/ Caribbean	7.9	6.8	6.1	6.2	4.6	3.4
North America	16.9	17.8	19.5	20.0	17.9	23.3
Europe	19.6	23.1	21.8	20.9	31.4	32.1
Oceania	3.3	3.9	3.9	3.9	3.1	3.3
Migrant Stock as a Percentage of Population						
World	2.3	2.1	2.2	2.3	2.9	2.9
Africa	2.5	2.7	2.3	2.5	2.6	2.1
Asia	1.7	1.3	1.4	1.4	1.6	1.4
Latin America/ Caribbean	2.4	1.8	1.6	1.7	1.6	1.1
North America	6.0	6.3	7.8	8.6	9.8	13.0
Europe	2.2	2.7	3.0	3.2	6.7	7.7
Oceania	14.4	15.6	16.9	17.8	18.0	19.1

SOURCE: Hatton and Williamson 2004, table 10.1.
NOTE: There are differences of definition in the figures for 1965–1990a and 1990b–2000, mainly involving the breakup of the Soviet Union.

TABLE 2

SOURCE-AREA COMPOSITION OF U.S. IMMIGRANTS, 1951–2000
(percent of total)

Region of Origin	1951–60	1961–70	1971–80	1981–90	1991–2000
Europe	52.7	33.8	17.8	10.3	14.9
West	47.1	30.2	14.5	7.2	5.6
East	5.6	3.6	3.3	3.1	9.4
Asia	6.1	12.9	35.3	37.3	30.7
Americas	39.6	51.7	44.1	49.3	49.3
Canada	15.0	12.4	3.8	2.1	2.1
Mexico	11.9	13.7	14.2	22.6	24.7
Caribbean	4.9	14.2	16.5	11.9	10.8
Central America	1.8	3.1	3.0	6.4	5.8
South America	3.6	7.8	6.6	6.3	5.9
Africa	0.6	0.9	1.8	2.4	3.9
Oceania	0.5	0.8	0.9	0.6	0.6
Total (thousands)	2,515	3,322	4,493	7,338	9,095

SOURCE: Hatton and Williamson 2004, table 10.2.
NOTES: National origin is based on country of last residence. Totals include 2.7 million former illegal aliens receiving permanent resident status under the Immigration Reform and Control Act, 1986. Of these, 1.3 million fall in the decade 1981–1990 and 1.4 million in the decade 1991–2000.

market quality of immigrants certainly has its parallel in the pre-1914 era, years that culminated in the influential Dillingham Commission Report in 1911 and the subsequent country-of-origin quotas imposed a decade later. An ominous comparison, perhaps, but it provides an obvious benchmark. So how do the two eras match up? In 1909, the wage for the average male immigrant in industry was 6.4 percent lower than for native-born men, a figure comparable with the late 1970s. Recent male immigrant arrivals in 1909 earned 20.4 percent less than natives, a figure also similar to the 1970s. But note this important fact: The variation in immigrant quality by source is *five times greater* in modern times than it was in the past—the standard deviation of the log wage across twenty-six immigrant nationalities was 0.056 in 1909 as compared with 0.295 across forty-one

immigrant nationalities in 1980.[1] Much of the source country difference in labor market performance is accounted for by the wage gap
between "old" and "new" immigrants. The wage gap in 1909 between
immigrants from northwest Europe (old) and the rest (new) was 6.7
percent. By contrast, the wage gap in 1980 between Europeans and
those from Africa, Asia, and South America was 30.7 percent.

The implication, of course, is that any shift in immigrant source
away from high-quality and toward low-quality origins has a much
bigger impact on the average quality of immigrants today than a
century ago. And so it was. Between 1873 and 1913, the effect of
changing source-country composition was to reduce the immigrant wage by 4.7 percentage points (2.3 percentage points after
1893). Between 1940 and 1980, source-country composition shifts
reduced the immigrant wage by 27 percentage points (17 percentage
points after 1960). So, while immigrants experienced an earnings disadvantage in 1980 similar in magnitude to that which prevailed on
the eve of World War I, the decline that preceded it was *much* larger
in the modern era and it continued for an additional decade as well.

In the earlier era, shifts in the source-country composition were
the result of rising incomes and demographic booms in Europe combined with falling transport costs between sending and receiving
regions, forces amplified by the friends and relatives effect. These
forces slowly reduced positive selection: The really poor could not
finance the move until late in the first global century, as their incomes
at home rose and the cost of passage fell (Hatton and Williamson
1998, chapter 3). The same forces have also been at work in the
modern era, but policy served to accelerate the demise of what the literature calls *positive selection*. These policy changes included the abo-
lition of the country-of-origin quotas that previously favored Europe,
the shift to a worldwide quota, and the emphasis on family reunification over skills as the key criteria for admission. Other OECD
countries also opened their doors more widely and experienced shifts
in immigrant composition and quality, but the effects have not been
as dramatic. For example, as the sources of Canadian immigration
widened after the 1960s, immigrant quality fell but by less than it did
in the United States (Baker and Benjamin 1994). Some have argued

that the difference can be explained by policy, the Canadian points system selecting immigrants with higher average labor quality (Borjas 1993). Perhaps, but note that the difference is accounted for by one dominant fact: Latin Americans are 47 percent of U.S. immigrants but only 14 percent of Canadian immigrants, and Mexicans account for most of that disparity (Antecol, Cobb-Clark, and Trejo 2003). While this Latin difference may be partly due to immigration policy, it also reflects location. Distance matters enormously in explaining who migrates to the United States (Clark, Hatton, and Williamson 2002). Because of its closer proximity to Latin America and its long land border with Mexico, the United States would need an even more skill-selective immigration policy than Canada (or even quotas for Latin Americans) to raise immigrant quality to the Canadian level.

What about the selection of immigrants from a given country? According to the Roy model, immigrants should be more negatively selected the higher is the return to skills (and the greater is earnings inequality) at the origin (Borjas 1987). Given that Mexican inequality exceeds American inequality, Mexican emigrants should be unskilled. So much for theory. In terms of observable skills, however, immigrants from Mexico were drawn predominantly from the *middle* of the distribution, not from the bottom (Chiquiar and Hanson 2002). A good example of this is offered by table 3, which reports education data for adult migrants in OECD host countries by sending source and for adults in the same sending source countries. While migrants in the OECD have 7.2 more years of education than the adults they left back home, Mexican migrants (mostly in the United States) had only 1.2 more years of education than did Mexican adults back home. The data in table 3 do not adjust for the fact that immigrants are younger than the average adult back home or that immigrants may have received some education in host countries after their arrival. However, it is very clear that the gap between mover and stayer is much smaller for Mexicans (close to the United States) and for East Europeans, Balkans, and Turks (close to the European Union). It appears that the revealed weaker positive selection is because, as a share of income, migration costs decrease sharply with skill level, offsetting the positive selection effects of greater inequality at the source.

TABLE 3
EDUCATION OF THOSE STAYING IN THE SENDING COUNTRY AND ITS
EMIGRANTS IN HOST COUNTRIES, C. 1990

Region (no. of sending countries)	Years of Schooling		
	Those Staying	Migrants to Host Countries	Difference (migrants -- stayers)
Africa (4)	4.6	15.4	10.8
Mexico (1)	6.3	7.5	1.2
Caribbean, Central America (14)	5.4	11.2	5.8
South America (10)	5.9	12.5	6.6
Asia (15)	5.8	14.4	8.6
Eastern Europe, Balkans, Turkey (3)	7.8	12.6	4.8
Total (47)	5.7	12.9	7.2

SOURCE: Based on Hendricks 2002, table B1.
NOTES: All figures are unweighted averages. The column of those who stayed is based on Barro-Lee, while the migrant column is based on OECD censuses around 1990. The two columns use country observations only if they supply information on both the stayers and the migrants.

Although Latin American immigrants are not, on the whole, negatively selected, it seems likely that they are less positively selected than migrants from poorer and more distant sources. To repeat, high migration costs favor positive selection and low migration costs favor negative selection. Mexico is close enough to the United States and countries to the immediate east and southeast are close enough to the EU, so that they all share lower migration costs and therefore can send poorer and less-skilled immigrants. Greater distances, lower source-country inequality, weaker friends and relatives effect, and (for the poorest regions) the poverty constraint all imply that U.S. and EU migrants coming from farther away should be more positively selected. So it was that the 1990 share of U.S. immigrants with tertiary schooling was more than three times higher for Asians and Africans than for Mexicans and Central Americans. One implication of this is that the brain drain must be more serious the poorer, the more distant, and the more egalitarian is the sending nation.

The United States faced rising immigrant quantity and falling immigrant quality before World War I, and it faces them again today. It appears that the same is true of the EU. What was the political economy of immigration backlash then? Do these lessons of history apply today?

A Framework

Most developed countries moved decisively to restrict immigration during the first third of the twentieth century. Those restrictive controls introduced between World War I and the 1930s were the result of a combination of factors: public assessment of the impact of immigration on the labor market, growth in the political participation of those affected, and as a triggering mechanism, the sudden shocks delivered by the 1890s depression, World War I, the postwar adjustment, and the 1930s depression. Public opinion was becoming increasingly negative toward immigration, in part as a response to the imagined or real economic threats delivered by immigration. When asked for their opinions by state labor bureau interviewers in the middle of the 1890s depression, here is how some workingmen in the Midwest responded: Almost 63 percent of the Kansas wage earners surveyed in 1895 thought immigration should be restricted and another 24 percent thought it should be outright suppressed, adding up to 87 percent who wanted to retreat from the free-immigration status quo; almost 68 percent of the Kansas wage earners surveyed in 1897 thought immigration should be restricted and another 24 percent thought it should be suppressed, adding up to 92 percent favoring a retreat from the status quo; about half the Michigan railway employees surveyed in 1895 thought that immigration injured their occupation; and almost 62 percent of the Michigan owners of public conveyances surveyed in 1895 thought immigration hurt their business through greater competition, and more than 92 percent favored restriction (Hatton and Williamson 2004, chapter 8).

Negative public opinion is on the rise today, too (Mayda 2003; O'Rourke and Sinnott 2004). A 1995 international survey asked whether immigration should be reduced in their country, where a score of 3 meant remain the same, 4 meant reduce a little, and 5 meant reduce a lot. The figures for three big immigrating countries were Germany 4.2, Britain 4.1, and the United States 3.9—ranging between "reduce a little" and "reduce a lot" (O'Rourke and Sinnott 2004, table 1). Furthermore, these responses were given during boom times in these labor markets. One can well imagine what they would be now, as the OECD struggles out of its recent slump. While the labor market effects of immigration are again at issue, fiscal effects matter now as well, and they matter far more today than a century ago when governments were much smaller and immigrants were never a big net fiscal burden. Nevertheless, the labor market effect of immigration has always been the key focus in debate over immigration policy, and it is what I focus on here.

The debate can be motivated by reference to the textbook picture of labor supply and demand in figure 1, where we simplify by assuming for the moment only one type of output and one type of labor. As usual, labor demand slopes downward to the right, capital and technology are taken to be fixed, and exogenous changes in immigration increase the total labor supply from S_1 to S_2. Immigration lowers the wage rate from W_1 to W_2 while it raises total profits from the area X to the area X + Y + Z (the area under the demand curve down to the wage). The total loss to resident wage earners is area Y and the net gain to society, excluding the immigrants themselves, is Z. Two points emerge immediately from figure 1. First, the overall gain to all residents collectively is likely to be small. One estimate for the United States puts the annual gain (Z) from the accumulated stock of immigrants at 0.1 percent of national income (Borjas 1999, 1701). Second, distributional effects are unambiguous—wage earners lose while their employers gain— and they are likely to be large. Immigration has different effects, therefore, on different interest groups, but if wage earners have the voting majority and immigration policy reflects majority preference, then policy is likely to be restrictive.[2]

FIGURE 1

THE ECONOMIC EFFECTS OF IMMIGRATION

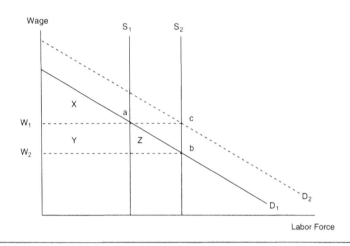

SOURCE: Hatton and Williamson 2004, table 14.1.

Things get more complicated the farther we depart from the assumptions underlying the simple textbook analysis underlying figure 1. Four complications are particularly important. First, if labor markets fail to clear through wage adjustment (in the short run at least), then immigrants add more to the labor force than to employment. If immigrants gain employment, they rob jobs from residents, pushing some of them into unemployment or out of the labor force. If, on the other hand, immigrants are the last hired and first fired, then the immigrants themselves dominate the unemployed, or the "informal," sector, where wages are more flexible and productivity lower. Second, labor market effects may be attenuated by adjustments in goods or capital markets. For example, if capital is the only other input and it is perfectly mobile internationally, then the new equilibrium in figure 1 is at c rather than b, as capital chases after the migrants in response to the incipient rise in returns (shifting the labor demand curve to the right from D_1 to D_2). Under perfect world capital mobility, and thus elastic capital supplies, the incomes of the domestic owners of capital and the wages of resident workers remain unchanged: Residents are neither better nor worse off, and the immigrants are absorbed without a hitch. Third, suppose there are two or more types of labor. If the immigrants are mainly unskilled, then unskilled residents may lose as a result of the increased job competition, but skilled workers may gain. The more are skilled and unskilled workers complements in production (and the less they are substitutes), the more likely skilled workers gain from unskilled immigration. Finally, some of the economic effects of immigration may come through fiscal transfer rather than labor market adjustment. If immigrants earn low wages and have low labor market participation, high unemployment, and high dependency rates, they are likely to be supported by residents through redistributive tax and welfare systems. If immigrants lack those attributes, then they are likely instead to support residents through transfers.

These are some of the more obvious effects of immigration on the incomes of resident populations. Listing them is easy enough; measuring them is not.

Looking at Local Labor Markets

One obvious way to measure the impact of immigration is to look across local labor markets that have different rates of immigration from abroad to see if those with higher rates of immigration also have slower wage or employment growth (or higher unemployment growth) among resident workers. One advantage of this so-called spatial correlations approach is that, by focusing on local labor markets *within* a nation, country-specific shocks and institutions are held constant. Because of these attractive features, a number of studies have employed this methodology to investigate the effects of immigration. The results of a representative sample of these are summarized in table 4, covering four OECD countries over the last four decades. The penultimate column reports the impact on wages in percent from an immigrant-induced 1-percent

TABLE 4

ESTIMATED EFFECTS OF IMMIGRATION ON WAGES AND
EMPLOYMENT OF NATIVES

Study	Country/Region, Time
Altonji and Card (1991)	U.S. cities, 1970–80
Lalonde and Topel (1991)	U.S. cities, 1970–80
Borjas, Freeman, and Katz (1997)	U.S. states, 1960–90 (men)
Card (2001)	U.S. cities, by occupation, 1985–90
De New and Zimmermann (1994)	German industries
Pischke and Velling (1997)	German counties, 1985–89
Addison and Worswick (2002)	Australian states, by occupation, 1982–96
Dustmann et al. (2002)	UK regions, 1983–2000

SOURCE: Hatton and Williamson 2004, table 14.1.
NOTE: The estimates reported here are based on regression coefficients that are often not significantly different from zero. Many of the authors offer a range of

change in the labor force. The last column reports the impact of the same immigrant-induced labor force impact on employment or unemployment, this in percentage points.

Table 4 makes it clear that there is little consensus among economists regarding the amount by which an immigrant influx (equivalent to 1 percent of the resident workforce) reduces the wage. In some cases, resident wages of the native born (and previous

Effect on Earnings of Equivalent to 1% of the Labor Force (percent)	Effect on Employment/Unemployment of Equivalent to 1% of the Labor Force (percentage points)
−1.2 (less skilled)	NA
−0.63 (immigrants); −0.83 (young blacks)	NA
0.59 (1960–70); 0.07 (1970–80); −0.01 (1980–90)	Employment: −0.03 (1960–1970); 0.13 (1970–1980); −0.05 (1980–1990)
−0.15	Employment: −0.05
−4.1 (all); −5.9 (blue collar); 3.5 (low-experienced white collar)	NA
NA	Employment: 0.05 Unemployment: 0.2
1.5 (all); 2.7 (less educated)	No effects on unemployment
1.9 (all); 2.2 (skilled); 1.2 (semiskilled); 2.2 (unskilled)	Unemployment: 0.2 (all); 0.1 (skilled); 0.4 (semiskilled); 0.03 (unskilled)

estimates using different methods, and the ones presented here are considered the most representative. Since the model specifications vary, the estimates from different studies are not strictly comparable.

immigrant cohorts) are reduced; in other cases, they are not. Lack of strong negative wage and crowding-out effects might be explained by the fact that, in the short run, immigration increases unemployment, as immigrants either "rob jobs" from locals or remain unemployed themselves. This impact would be expected if wage rates are sticky downward, as we think they are in the short run. However, there is no consistent evidence confirming adverse effects on employment or unemployment in local labor markets.

Findings like these contributed to a general consensus by the mid-1990s that the effects of immigration on host country labor markets are small (Borjas 1994; Friedberg and Hunt 1995). Yet, three nagging doubts suggested that the "small-impact" view was premature. First, the finding that immigration neither reduces the wage nor raises unemployment seems to be inconsistent with elementary theory: Labor demand curves slope downward to the right. It seems justified to insist that analysts offer an explicit explanation for any finding that rejects such a powerful weapon from the economists' arsenal. Furthermore, such findings are inconsistent with decades of empirical work by economists who estimated the labor demand curve to have elasticities around −0.5 or higher (Hammermesh 1993). Second, there is little consistency across these modern immigration studies, even for the same country. Third, economists have ignored the first global century and that pre–World War I history shows unambiguously that immigrants crowded out natives.

So where has the modern economist gone wrong? There are several reasons why the spatial correlation approach is biased against finding large crowding-out effects. One reason is simply that the annual flow of immigration is usually small relative to the size of the labor market. Since immigrants gravitate toward a few major urban centers, most regions in most countries that make up the bulk of the observations in local area studies have immigrant inflows that are very small relative to local labor supply. Nearly a third of the U.S. foreign born live in just three metropolitan areas: New York, Los Angeles, and Miami. About 40 percent of immigrants to Britain go to London alone and the same share of immigrants to Australia go to Sydney, while more than a third of those arriving in France locate in the greater Paris area. Hence, systematic immigration effects are hard to assess anywhere but in the few areas where new immigrants concentrate. To make matters worse, immigrants tend to locate in areas where economic conditions are favorable: where unemployment is low and falling and wages are high and rising.

Local immigration is, at least in part, endogenous; and where immigration is endogenous, the direction of causation is reversed and of the opposite sign. When both this endogenous effect and the "true" labor market impact are present, the net result is to bias estimates of crowding out downward. That downward bias could be big.

More important still, the markets for labor and goods are likely to be very well integrated within developed countries, much more so than between countries. Suppose goods markets adjust quickly: As immigrants are absorbed in one region, it expands its production of the goods that use most intensively the skills that immigrants bring. In short, a boom in the region's export sector absorbs the immigrants. Labor markets are also likely to be far better integrated within a country than between countries. As immigrants enter a local labor market, they induce interregional migration by the native born and previous immigrant cohorts with whom they compete. As a result, the crowding-out effect is not observed accurately at the local level. Indeed, it may not be observed at all. Integrated national goods and labor markets imply that the effects of immigration are spread across the entire country: All boats rise and fall together as the immigrant tide flows and ebbs. The better integrated are the markets for goods and labor across regions within a country, the less is an immigration shock reflected in local labor markets, even though the effects of immigration could still be large for the country as a whole.

If regional markets are well integrated, then the effects of immigration can be observed only at the national level. But how? George Borjas (2003) argued recently that if different types of labor (defined by schooling and labor market experience) are not good substitutes for each other, then the effects of immigration can be inferred by estimating the relative wage impacts of changes in the supply of different types of labor at the national level. One advantage of this approach is that mobility between these skill groups is limited. Intercensal changes between 1960 and 2000 reveal strong negative effects consistent with labor demand elasticities ranging between –0.3 and –0.4, a little below the –0.5 elasticity typically found for labor demand. Therefore, the 11 percent increase in labor supply brought about by immigration between 1980 and 2000 must have reduced the wage of the average nonimmigrant worker by 3.2 percent. Not surprisingly, these impacts vary greatly across the skill groups: Immigration reduced the wage by 8.9 percent for high school dropouts, 4.9 percent for college graduates, 2.6 percent for high school graduates, and almost nothing for those with some college education (Borjas 2003, 36). Thus, to the extent that immigrants cluster in the group competing with high school dropouts, the crowding-out impact is very big (bringing that elasticity closer to –0.5). As we shall see, this result is consistent with assessments of immigration's impact on host labor markets during the age of mass migration before World War I.

An alternative approach is to look across countries whose labor markets are linked only very loosely. One recent study examined the short-run impact of immigration on native employment rates in eighteen European countries between 1983 and 1999, using the "shock" of asylum immigrants from Eastern Europe to better identify the effects (Angrist and Kugler 2003). The study found that the addition of one hundred immigrants to a country's labor force reduced native employment by between thirty-five and eighty-five, for an average of sixty (close again to that –0.5 elasticity). These job losses were largest for young men; and overall job loss was greater in countries with the least flexible labor markets and the highest benefit replacement rates (for example, the European welfare states). It seems reasonable to conclude that the initial effects on employment would eventually translate into wage effects, the adjustment process depending on the degree of labor market flexibility.

These new findings seem to have solved the riddle of why the modern, spatial correlation approach so often fails to find big negative immigration effects on either wage rates or resident employment. Immigrants *do* lower the incomes of those residents with whom they compete most directly, just as they did a century ago. But why did the spatial correlation approach fail to find big labor market effects? Was it goods market integration, labor market integration, or something else? Let us begin with the goods market.

The Rybczynski theorem suggests that a globally integrated region can absorb changes in relative factor supply without changes in relative factor prices (in this case, wages relative to other factor prices). As noted previously, when unskilled immigrants arrive in a local market, the theorem predicts a relative expansion of industries that use the additional unskilled labor most intensively and a shift in the pattern of trade with other regions toward exporting those goods that use the newly abundant factor most intensively. A recent study isolated these effects by looking at the skill composition across forty industries in fourteen U.S. states. The study found that a significant part of the difference across states in their skill mix was accounted for by changes in their output mix "consistent with the hypothesis that state-specific factor-supply shocks do not trigger large state-specific wage effects" (Hanson and Slaughter 2003, 19).[3] While these results offer an impressive confirmation of market integration among U.S. states, they do not tell us whether the goods market or the labor market does the adjusting. So, let us turn to the labor market.

In April 1980, Fidel Castro declared that Cubans were free to emigrate from the port of Mariel. In just a few months, 125,000 took up Castro's offer and about half of these settled in Miami. The Cuban influx added 7 percent to the Miami labor force, and they were mainly unskilled. In his celebrated study of this Mariel boatlift, David Card (1990) found that this large Cuban influx had almost no effect on the wage rates of the unskilled relative to skilled in Miami or relative to the wage rates of the unskilled in other states. Even previous cohorts of Cubans and other Hispanics did not seem to have suffered from competition with the Marielitos. Why? It looks like the answer is displacement. In-migration to Miami of the native born (or previous immigrants) slowed down dramatically in the early 1980s, so much so that interregional migration accounted for most of the adjustment.

How general are the Mariel findings? Is the interregional displacement effect of natives by immigrants large at the economywide level? One post-Mariel study found that an influx of immigrants 1975–80 equivalent to 1 percent of a standard metropolitan statistical area's labor force displaced native workers equivalent to 1.2 percent of the labor force (Filer 1992). This huge displacement—more than one for one—seems consistent with the Miami experience following the Mariel boatlift. Looking at intercensal *changes* in the growth of native and foreign-born populations in U.S. states, another study also found a crowding-out effect close to one (Borjas et al. 1997). Other studies have reported much more modest effects (Card 2001).

This variety in results is hardly unique to the United States, and it may be due in part to some of the same problems that beset the spatial correlations studies of local employment and wage rates. That is, when immigration to most of the regions in a sample is small, measurement error or idiosyncratic shocks to a regional labor supply or demand may obscure the immigration crowding-out effect. To illustrate the point, consider the net interregional migration into six booming regions in the south of the United Kingdom from 1982 to 2000. One study explained that interregional migration by regional job vacancy rates, earnings, and house prices as well as by the net foreign immigration into the region (Hatton and Tani 2003, table 5). The study found that, for every hundred foreign immigrants, forty-three residents were displaced from the region. But when the relationship is assessed for all eleven U.K. regions, not just those six in the booming south, the foreign immigration impact falls in size and becomes insignificant. It appears that the total immigration effect is now harder to discern because the additional five regions received relatively few migrants.

Similar effects can be observed for other times and places, provided that the regions observed are ones where immigration has been large. In the decades before 1910, the bulk of immigrants to the United States moved into New England, the mid-Atlantic, and the east north central. An analysis of the intercensal flows of native born from the fourteen states that compose those three regions showed that crowding-out occurred there, too. Indeed, the westward migration in the United States was powerfully influenced by the influx of foreign immigrants into the East. For every net inflow of one hundred immigrants, the out-migration of native born increased by forty (Hatton and Williamson 1998, 168). This late nineteenth century estimate is very close to the late twentieth century estimate for contemporary southern Britain just discussed. The similarity serves to reinforce the point that the crowding-out effects of immigration can be observed only by focusing on times and places where immigration has been large, so that its effects can be clearly assessed.

Immigration Shocks and Labor Market Absorption: Two Modern Examples

Perhaps a better way to assess the effects of immigration on the host economy is to look at what might be called *natural experiments,* cases (like the Mariel boatlift) where the changes in immigration have been sudden and unambiguously exogenous and where they are large enough to leave a clear imprint on the whole country's labor market. This section considers two modern examples: the migration of Soviet Jews to Israel in the early 1990s after Soviet emigration policy became liberal and the return migration of French Algerians to metropolitan France in 1962 following independence.

The dramatic influx of immigrants into Israel in the early 1990s offers a classic example of an exogenous immigration shock of significant economywide proportions (Cohen and Hsieh 2000; Eckstein and Weiss 2003). Late in 1989, the government of what was then the Soviet Union shifted its policy to permit Soviet Jews to emigrate. Most of those who left went to Israel. The dramatic surge in Israel's aggregate immigration rate is shown in figure 2. In the decade before 1990, it averaged 3.7 per thousand of the Israeli population. In 1990–91, the rate surged to more than thirty-five per thousand and then continued at ten to fifteen per thousand for the rest of the decade. There was an inflow of 610,000 in the first two years, equivalent to 7 percent of the Israeli population, and by the mid-1990s, the influx amounted to a million, or about 12 percent of the initial population. The effects on the labor market were equally dramatic: The working age population increased by 8 percent between 1990 and 1992 and by 16 percent up to 1997.

FIGURE 2
IMMIGRATION TO ISRAEL, 1980–2000
(per 1,000 population)

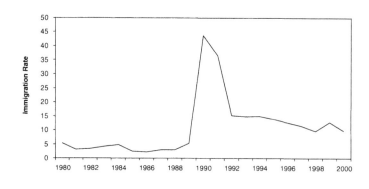

SOURCE: Israel, Central Statistical Bureau online at http://194.90.153.197/reader/
shnatonenew.htm.

An exogenous immigration shock of this magnitude should have
left a clear mark on the host country labor market, and figure 3
confirms that this was so. The figure plots percentage deviations
from logarithmic trends calculated for the preshock period,
1980–89. The labor force was more than 15 percent above its trend
by the mid-1990s. Employment rose more slowly at first, but by the
mid-1990s, it was more than 20 percent above its trend. Relative to
its trend, the real wage plunged in the early 1990s, then hovered at
about 10 percent below the trend for the rest of the decade. There
were other short-run adjustments as well. The unemployment rate
was 10.6 percent in 1991, compared with an average of 6.1 percent
over the 1980s. Furthermore, the unemployment rate was 37.3
percent among immigrants, compared with 9 percent among
nonimmigrants. This difference evaporated over the 1990s, and by
2000, it was just two percentage points apart, 10.4 percent for
immigrants and 8.4 percent for nonimmigrants.

The Israeli evidence seems clear: The real wage fell by around
5 percent for every 10 percent immigration-induced increase in the

FIGURE 3
LABOR SUPPLY AND THE REAL WAGE IN ISRAEL, 1980–2000
(deviations from 1980–89 trend)

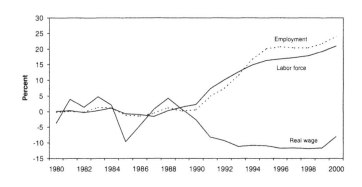

SOURCE: Bank of Israel online at http://www.bankisrael.gov.il/publeng/dataeng.htm.

labor force—once again, that elasticity of about –0.5. But other forces at work helped ease the labor market adjustment. One was an impressive capital accumulation response. The sudden increase in labor supply reduced the capital/labor ratio and increased the return to capital; as a result, gross investment in machinery and equipment increased from 12 percent of the stock in the 1980s to 19 percent in 1994–1996. This accumulation response was financed largely from abroad; as a share of the GDP, the current account deficit increased by about 8 percentage points between 1990 and 1996 (Cohen and Hsieh 2000, 19). In contrast, adjustments through induced changes in the composition of output and the structure of trade do not seem to have been important. Although immigrants were more highly skilled than natives, no shift in the output composition toward skill-intensive sectors took place (Cohen and Hsieh 2000, 15).

Given that immigrants *appeared* to enter with much higher skill levels and the lack of adjustment in the output mix, one might have anticipated a big fall in the premium for skill. Appearances can be deceiving. Among those Soviet Jews arriving in the first wave, 60 percent were college educated and 25 percent were college graduates, compared with 30 percent and 12 percent, respectively, of Israeli Jews. They also had much higher occupation-specific skills. Of those arriving in 1990–93, 57,000 had been engineers and 12,000 had been physicians; by comparison, the numbers in the much bigger 1989 Israeli labor force were 30,000 and 15,000, respectively. Therefore, given the higher skills of the immigrants, one might have expected the skill premium to fall. In fact, it *increased* (very slightly) to the mid-1990s, before it fell back, largely because the Russian immigrants entered occupational grades that were considerably below those in which they had worked previously. Looking across occupations, there is a negative correlation between the number of Russian entrants and wage growth between 1989 and 1994: Every 10 percent added to employment reduced the wage by 3–6 percent—once again, implying an elasticity of almost –0.5. But there is no correlation between the number of Russians classified by *former* occupation and wage growth in that occupation (Friedberg 2001). Hence, in 1994, the Russian immigrant earned 45 percent less than the Israeli despite having an average of one more year of schooling. There are two important explanations for this downgrading. First, education and skills acquired in Russia were not easily transferable to the Israeli labor market, and second, many of the immigrants had poor Hebrew language skills. The assimilation process took time, but the Soviet immigrants did move up the Israeli occupational ladder, and by 1997, they had about the same occupational distribution as the Israeli labor force as a whole.

The second modern example is offered by the inflow to metropolitan France from Algeria following the latter's independence. These immigrants were very largely French-born expatriates fleeing the regime change; about 900,000 flooded into France in the year 1962. They added about 1.9 percent to the population and 1.6 percent to the labor force. They were slightly younger and better qualified on average than the host labor force, but those differences were not large. They located largely in southern France. An analysis of changes in average earnings across departments between 1962 and

1967 indicates that an influx of repatriates equivalent to 1 percent of the French labor force reduced the wage by 0.5–0.8 percent (Hunt 1992, 567)—once again, an elasticity around –0.5 or more. The overall effect was to reduce the wage by 1.3 percent and increase unemployment rates by 0.3 percentage points. In short, the Algerian immigration shock was sufficiently large to have a clear effect on French labor markets.

Immigrants, Wages, and Inequality: The Global Centuries Compared

How has immigration affected incomes and income distributions in the larger economies, such as the United States, that received the bulk of migrant flows from the less-developed parts of the world? And how do these effects compare with those we observe for the first global century before 1914? The French and Israeli examples suggest that, when the impact on the host country labor supply is large enough to observe the impact clearly, the effects of immigration accord with the simple model depicted in figure 1. Given that accordance, the wider effects of immigration can be easily calculated.

Using a standard production function that combines capital with different types of labor, the effects on the earnings of workers of different skills arising from immigrant-induced changes in labor supply by skill can be estimated (Borjas et al. 1997). Assuming capital to be fixed, the effects of U.S. immigration between 1979 and 1995 were to reduce the earnings of skilled natives by 2.5 percent and the unskilled native born by 4.6 percent. Immigration therefore contributed to a rise in U.S. earnings inequality, the earnings ratio of the skilled to the unskilled having increased by 2.1 percent. If instead perfect world capital mobility is assumed (capital flows into the U.S. economy in response to immigration, keeping the rate of return constant), then earnings for skilled natives now actually increase (although only slightly) while those of unskilled natives fall by 4.6 percent as before. Therefore, the earnings ratio of the skilled to the unskilled increases by more (5 percent) when there is perfect world capital mobility and hence elastic capital supplies. Because the bulk of the labor force is skilled, and capital and skilled labor are assumed to be complementary, the average wage falls only marginally when there is perfect world capital mobility. The gain to the economy as a whole (area Z in figure 1) is at most 0.1 percent of the GDP.

How do these estimated modern labor market impacts compare with the late nineteenth century estimates? Had there been no U.S. immigration over the forty years between 1870 and 1910, it has been estimated that the unskilled real wage would have been higher in 1910 by 34 percent, a figure that falls to 9.2 percent if perfect world capital mobility is assumed (Taylor and Williamson 1997; Hatton and Williamson 1998, chapter 8; O'Rourke and Williamson 1999, chapter 8). While these late nineteenth century impact estimates are double those of the late twentieth century (9.2 versus 4.6), the former covers a much longer period, when immigration rates were much higher, too. Suppose we focus instead on the 1870–90 decades, a shorter period with lower immigration rates. In this case, the 1890 real wage would have been higher by 14.4 percent in the absence of immigration and by only 3.7 percent if capital mobility is assumed (Hatton and Williamson 1998, 212). While the estimates for the late nineteenth century are derived differently from those for the late twentieth century, they appear to fall into the same ballpark (3.7 versus 4.6), at least when perfect world capital mobility is assumed.

There is a moral here that is worth stressing. Immigrant absorption is much easier in times when world capital markets are globally integrated. Under such conditions, world capital is allowed to chase after world migrations, augmenting the capacity of the host country to absorb the immigrants. Complaints about crowding-out and evidence of rising inequality are muted under such conditions, conditions satisfied before 1913 and after 1970. They were not satisfied between 1913 and 1970, when world capital markets were in a shambles.

This analysis of two U.S. immigration periods separated by a century ignores some important differences in the character of the immigration and the structure of the economy—differences that should have mattered to the economywide impact. First, the late twentieth century skill gap between immigrants and natives was *five times larger* than in the late nineteenth century; hence, the immigrants' influence on reducing the host country skill mix—diluting its "quality"—should have been much greater in more recent times. Added to that, the unskilled are now a much smaller share of the U.S. labor force, and so a given immigrant inflow should make a proportionately larger contribution to the unskilled labor supply. Hence, the effects of immigration on the unskilled wage should be even greater today than they were a century ago. However, these forces have a potential offset, the absorptive capacity of the U.S. economy. Consider that agricultural employment, where labor was unskilled, accounted for 50 percent of the U.S. labor force in 1870 and 27 percent in 1913 but only 3 percent in 1999. How does this fact speak to the labor absorption issue (Williamson 1982)? Land was a much more important factor of production a century ago—and land is a quasi-fixed factor. Given the importance of land, there were much stronger economywide diminishing returns to a rising unskilled labor force in the nineteenth century, effects that were only partly ameliorated by international capital mobility. For this reason, the same immigrant inflow had larger effects on unskilled earnings in the nineteenth century than it does today. Apparently trends in these two offsetting forces (a rising skill gap between immigrant and native born *versus* an improved capacity to absorb the immigrant) have been pretty much a wash, since the net effect of the two is similar then and now.

Policy and the Demise of Mass Migration in the First Global Century

World War I brought an end to mass migration and closed the door on the first global century. The combined effects of two world wars, the Great Depression, and the introduction of a restrictive immigration policy served to choke off emigration to the New World, and those mass migrations never regained their pre-1914 levels in the half century that followed. What was true of absolute levels was even more true, of course, of migration rates.

The magnitude of the collapse in the global mass migrations is apparent in figures 4 and 5, both based on the impressive work of Dudley Kirk (1946) alone and that involving the famous collaboration between Imre Ferenczi and Walter Willcox (1929), scholars who lived through the global implosion between 1914 and 1950. Three central facts leap out from those two figures. First, the migrations of the 1920s were never able to recover the migrations of the 1880s, let alone those of 1895–1914, and they fell to much lower levels after the 1920s. By the 1950s, the United States was no longer a melting pot or a nation of immigrants but rather a closed economy whose youth was mostly native born, a characteristic that fit awkwardly on the shoulders of this new twentieth-century world leader. Second, most of the collapse was due to the sharp decline in emigration from the new source countries located in southern and eastern Europe: the Austro-Hungarian Empire, the Russian Empire, Iberia, Italy, and the Balkans. Emigration from the old sources in northwestern Europe— the British Isles, Scandinavia, the Lowlands, Germany, France, and Switzerland—fell hardly at all. Third, the United States underwent the biggest fall in immigration, far exceeding that of the other top three overseas destinations: Argentina, Brazil, and Canada.

When the guns of August started thundering in 1914, European immigration to the New World began to dry up: Overseas immigration to the United States fell from 1.1 million annually in both 1913 and 1914 to 60,000 and 54,000 in 1918 and 1919 (figure 5). Potential immigrants in the European interior found it difficult to make their way to the traditional ports of departure, and ports shut down to commercial activity, making steerage space scarce and expensive. As the war in the trenches dragged on, economic hardship made it increasingly difficult for potential emigrants in source countries to find the resources to finance the move. Postwar recession and unemployment kept the figures low in 1919 and 1920. With economic recovery in 1921, the United States recorded an overseas immigration rate of 702,000, as high

FIGURE 4
EMIGRATION FROM EUROPE, 1871–1939
(five-year averages)

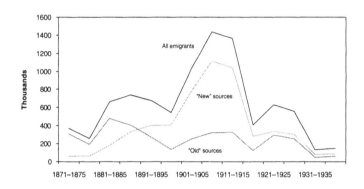

SOURCE: Kirk 1946, p. 289.

FIGURE 5
IMMIGRATION INTO CHIEF NEW WORLD DESTINATIONS, 1881–1939

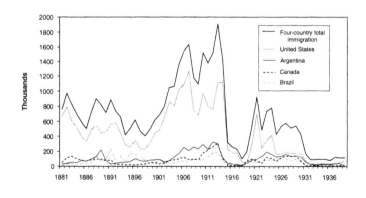

SOURCE: Ferenczi and Willcox 1929, pp. 361, 384–89, 539–40, 550; Kirk 1946, p. 280.

TABLE 5

NET U.S. IMMIGRATION BY REGION OF ORIGIN, 1910–1939

	1910–19	1920–29	1930–39
"Old" Europe	910,309 (21.2%)	991,128 (32.9%)	77,839 (37.0%)
"New" Europe	2,548,453 (59.5%)	542,058 (18.0%)	113,016 (53.7%)
Mexico	135,678 (3.2%)	455,502 (15.1%)	−75,240 (−35.8%)
Canada	417,016 (9.7%)	912,651 (30.3%)	144,325 (68.6%)
Other	274,809 (6.4%)	107,441 (3.6%)	−49,503 (−23.5%)
Total	4,286,265 (100.0%)	3,008,780 (100.0%)	210,437 (100.0%)

SOURCE: Gemery 1994, table 9.2, 178.
NOTE: Canada includes Newfoundland.

as anything achieved over the fifteen years between 1885 and 1900, but that brief spurt was it. The average between 1922 and 1929 was 232,000, a figure about one-third the 1881–1914 average. During the Great Depression decade, the flood dried up to a trickle, averaging about 50,000 each year. The great mass migration was over.

How much of this collapse in European emigration was due to policy and how much to war and the Great Depression? It seems quite clear that, in the short run, much of the collapse in global migration can be attributed to world wars and the Great Depression. The clearest evidence of this fact is that none of the country quotas was binding from the early 1930s to the mid-1940s. Although the country quotas were set far below pre-1914 immigration levels, the new regions of emigration were able to fill only small shares of their quotas between 1932 and 1937: southern and eastern Europe, less than 40 percent; Asia, less than 30 percent; and Africa, less than 10 percent (Gemery 1994, figure 9.1). However, two lessons of history apply here. First, changes in immigration policy usually come in very big, discrete steps, and only after long, acrimonious, and time-intensive debates (Timmer and Williamson 1998). The U.S. debate started on the House floor in 1895, continued with the first House roll call in 1897, when

86 percent of the representatives voting went for restriction, continued still further with the creation of the fact-finding Immigration (Dillingham) Commission in 1906, and concluded with the 1917 congressional override of Woodrow Wilson's veto. The fact that the policy steps are big when implemented maximizes their impact at the destination. Second, when the underlying fundamentals favor immigration restrictions, usually they are not imposed until an economic crisis occurs, when short-run labor market problems are most apparent and affected citizens are most verbal. These are precisely the episodes when labor demand slumps, labor markets go slack, potential emigrants postpone their move, and previous immigrants return home disappointed. Net immigration falls to low levels, even in the absence of any policy restriction. Hence, the impact of immigration restrictions must be assessed over the long run, when capacity rather than aggregate demand determines output, employment, and productivity and when peacetime normalcy rather than wartime scarcities dominates.

Four pieces of U.S. immigration legislation were enacted over the decade 1917–27, and all were restrictive in intent and impact.[4]

The 1917 Immigration Act imposed a literacy test that was precisely the instrument of restriction debated by Congress from 1895 onward. By the end of World War I, the literacy test proved completely ineffective in stemming the inflow, mainly because, while the U.S. Congress was debating, a revolution in the provision of free and public elementary education was spreading east and south to backward and illiterate Europe (Easterlin 1981; Lindert 2003). Italy illustrates the process best. Between 1881 and 1931, Italian regional literacy rates soared: from less than 20 percent to more than 60 percent in southern Italy, Sicily, and Sardinia; from less than 35 percent to almost 80 percent in central Italy; from about 40 percent to about 85 percent in Venice and Emilia; and from almost 60 percent to more than 95 percent in the northern industrial triangle (Kirk 1946, 183–85). The literacy rate for Italy as a whole was about 80 percent by 1931. What about the rest of poor Europe, and what about young adults whose literacy is much more relevant evidence for any prediction regarding the effectiveness of the 1917 literacy act? The literacy rate in poor European source countries (including Italy) for those aged 15–29 ranged from 80 to 83 percent in 1931 (Kirk 1946, table 12, 189). No wonder the literacy criteria failed to offer an effective bar to immigrants from poor European countries. However, the 1917 legislation *did* include an "Asian barred zone" provision that was very effective in keeping out almost all potential immigrants from that part of the world.

The second piece of restrictive legislation was the Emergency Quota Act of 1921 (the Johnson Act) that set limits to immigration from Eastern Hemisphere countries. This second act was implemented in a congressional rush, when the 702,000 arrived from Europe that year (easily jumping over the literacy bar) and with the election of President Warren Harding, who was much more comfortable with anti-immigration interests than his predecessor, Woodrow Wilson. The annual number of immigrants of a given nationality was limited to no more than 3 percent of that nationality as recorded in the 1910 Census. Under the 1921 act, quotas for immigrants from northern and western Europe were set at about 198,000, and from all other source countries, mainly southern and eastern Europe, at about 158,000, or about 356,000 in all. The legislation was clearly targeted to limit "new" immigrants who, the prewar Dillingham Immigration Commission had argued, were harder to assimilate, were a source of poverty and a potential welfare burden on the state, became poor citizens, or failed to become citizens at all. That is, it targeted "low-quality" immigrants. The targets worked: Annual quotas for southern and eastern European countries were in all cases less than a quarter the numbers admitted before the war. The Asian "barred zone" remained in place, a racial restriction that applied everywhere in overseas destination countries, including Australia, Brazil, Canada, and Natal. This Asian restriction embedded in the U.S. acts had its source in the increasingly strong lobbying interests on the West Coast who managed to get Congress to accept a Chinese exclusion act as early as 1882. Had British Columbia, California,

Nevada, Oregon, and Washington formed an independent nation in 1870, the New World would have seen an Asian exclusion act even sooner. Furthermore, U.S. Asian restrictions stayed in place for almost a century, until the reforms of 1965.

The 1921 act also had a pro–Western Hemisphere bias since such immigration was not subject to quotas. After all, there appeared to be no reason to set quotas since South America seemed too poor and too distant to become a viable pool of emigrants, at least not yet. Furthermore, Canada was viewed as a member of the British family with old European origins. Finally, farm interests in the Southwest were lobbying for cheap Mexican unskilled labor to work their fields, the products of which were now supplying national and international markets. These aspects had one important, but perhaps unpredictable, implication. Illegal immigrants poured over the border from Canada and Mexico, trying to sidestep the European quotas and the Asian restrictions by passing through contiguous neighbors and over porous borders. One estimate has it that "hundreds of thousands (perhaps millions) of illegal immigrants" entered the United States in the 1920s via Canada and Mexico (Briggs 1984, 48). In any case, the share of (legal) U.S. immigrants coming from Canada and Mexico rose from 12.9 percent in 1910–19 to 45.4 percent in 1920–29. Mexican immigration by itself rose by about 320,000 over the decade (table 5), a harbinger of things to come later in the century.

Finally, the 1921 act also introduced a nonquota category. This category was based on individual characteristics (rather than nationality) and would come to represent the "family reunification" part of U.S. immigration.

The 1921 act was not restrictive enough for some anti-immigration interests, and their power in Congress was on the rise. Therefore, the 1924 (Johnson-Reid) act lowered the quota from 356,000 to 165,000, mostly by reducing the new source country quota from 158,000 to 21,000 (Bernard 1982, table 3.1, 96). The more restrictive quotas were now set at 2 percent of the foreign born by nationality in the 1890 Census. The 1927 act completed a decade of U.S. experimentation with immigration restriction, ending with what has been called a *national origins act*, which set the overall quota at about 150,000, now based on national origins of the U.S. 1920 population.

Recall that there were quota and nonquota categories, and the 1924 act made it far easier for relatives to enter as nonquota immigrants. Since wives and children were now exempted from the numerical quota, the number admitted each year from a given country in the late 1920s was much higher than that set by the quota. Thus, actual gross immigration into the United States from southern and eastern Europe was more than three times the quota in 1929 (Gemery 1994, table 9.4, 182).

Family reunification had become an important part of U.S. immigration policy by the late 1920s, and it was reinforced in the 1965 reforms. It has stayed that way ever since. Indeed, who did the U.S. quotas keep out and what did it do to positive selection? As table 5 shows, net immigration to the United States fell dramatically from 4.3 million in 1910–19 to 210,000 in 1930–39. But the composition by source also changed dramatically, reflecting the intent of the legislation. The share coming from "new" sources in Europe fell from almost 60 percent in the 1910s to 18 percent in the 1920s, and the share from "other" (mainly Asia) fell from 6.4 to 3.6 percent over the same period. In short, traditional "low-quality" sources ("new" Europe and Asia) dropped from 65.9 to 21.6 percent of the total immigration. In contrast, the "old" European and Canadian share combined rose from 30.9 to 63.2 percent.

These national-origins policies clearly increased positive selection to the extent that a larger share of U.S. immigrants was coming from developed regions. Indeed, the share of immigrants entering with skilled, professional, or commercial occupations rose from 17.9 percent in 1911–16 to 24.1 percent in 1926–30 and 30.6 percent in 1936–40 (Gemery 1994, 178). Among those in the labor force and hence reporting occupations, the rise is even more dramatic, from 24.6 to 40.4 and to 69.1 percent. To repeat, the intent of the quotas was achieved: Immigrants from "low-quality" sending regions fell dramatically. But we now know that the "quality" gap between the "old" and the "new" European immigrants was actually pretty small: In 1909, the wage gap between old and new immigrants in U.S. labor markets was only 6.7 percent (Hatton 2000)! Contemporary observers acted like that quality gap was much bigger, perhaps because they had not given the "new" immigrants the same opportunity to assimilate that had already been given to the "old" immigrants. In any case, it is hard to believe that the quotas really served to increase U.S. labor market skills by much, even though it certainly did have a big impact on immigrant by source.

Note, however, the impact of family reunification. The share of female immigrants rose from 35.1 to 54.8 percent over the two decades, almost a 20 percentage point rise; and the share of individuals not in the labor force (mainly women and children) rose from 27.2 to 55.7 percent, a 28.5 percentage point rise. In short, it looks like a century of positive selection—carrying high labor participation rates and low dependency rates overseas—was completely overturned by policies introduced during the quota decade. Oddly enough, economic historians of the first global century and modern analysts of the second global century have not paid much attention to this fact, perhaps because politicians have always found "cheap labor from poor countries" good rhetoric when seeking votes from the working man.

Population and Labor Force Impact of the Quotas

Did the collapse in world migration have an impact on receiving countries? The United States was the biggest immigrant labor market and it also underwent the biggest decline in immigration after 1914, so our focus is there. Whether due to a switch to a restrictive immigration policy, war, the Great Depression, or all three in concert, did the rate of labor force and population growth slow down in the three decades after World War I? If so, how much of the decline can be attributed to declining immigration? Only if we can show that the immigration policy switch contributed to a labor force slowdown can we then ask whether it had an impact on economic events within the U.S. economy.

Three studies explored the impact of immigration on the U.S. population and labor supply in the interwar years, but all three seem to have asked the wrong question. Simon Kuznets and Ernest Rubin (1954) adopted a foreign-born measure and counted net migrants of labor force age and immigrant children born abroad as they reached employment age. Richard Easterlin's (1968) measure was narrower, and excluded the impact of immigrant children. More recently, Henry Gemery (1994) extended the analysis, also using the Easterlin measure, the narrow definition that we use in what follows. However, all three studies measured only the share of the observed labor force or population increases accounted for by *observed* immigration. While such accounting decompositions are useful, they do not assess the impact of the demise of mass migration on labor force or population growth. What we want instead is to compare what we observe with a counterfactual world in which the mass migrations continued. Only then can we identify the role of the demise of mass migration.

First, what was the extent of the labor force slowdown? Table 6 documents a dramatic fall in the rate of labor force growth in the United States, from 2.29 percent per annum over the three prewar decades, 1880–1910, to 1.14 percent per annum over the three war and interwar decades, 1910–40. This slowdown in the rate of labor supply growth amounted to 1.15 percentage points, a massive regime switch in which the growth rate was cut in half. Would we find similar large numbers for other immigrant countries? The answer depends on two factors. First, which economies were most dependent on immigration prior to World War I? We already know the answer to that question: Immigration after 1870 raised the 1910 labor force of Argentina by 86 percent, Canada by 44 percent, Australia by 42 percent, and the United States by 24 percent (Taylor and Williamson 1997). Second, which economies underwent the biggest fall in mass migration? With an answer in hand, we would then predict that the biggest labor force slowdown occurred in those economies where net

TABLE 6

U.S. LABOR FORCE GROWTH, 1910–1940: SOME COUNTERFACTUALS

	Labor Force Growth Rate (% per annum)	Percentage Due to Net Immigration
Actual: 1880–1910	2.29	40.1
Actual: 1910–40	1.14	11.6
Counterfactuals for 1910–40 with Immigrant Participation Rate of 1910–40		
Net immigration rate of 1910–40	1.14	11.6
Absolute net immigration of 1880–1910	1.38	30.9
Net immigration rate of 1880–1910	1.66	44.1
Counterfactuals for 1910–40 with Immigrant Participation Rate of 1880–1910		
Net immigration rate of 1910–40	1.17	14.5
Absolute net immigration of 1880–1910	1.48	35.6
Net immigration rate of 1880–1910	1.82	50.4

SOURCE: Hatton and Williamson 2004, table 9.3.

migration had the biggest impact on the prewar labor force totals and across-border net migration underwent the biggest decline after 1914. Australia would be one such candidate; indeed, the rate of labor force growth there fell by 1.41 percentage points between 1870–1913 and 1913–38 (Maddison 1991, 266). The other immigrant countries are harder to document, but we expect similar answers.

Next, does the demise of mass migration explain the slowdown? Table 6 poses the following counterfactual: What would have been the rate of labor force growth between 1910 and 1940 had the 1880–1910 immigration experience persisted? Our expectations are, of course, that the demise in the mass migrations accounted for a very large share of the slowdown in labor force growth. The counterfactuals are calculated to take account of two forces. First, immigration into the United States fell after 1910. So, what would have been the impact on 1910–40 if, first, the immigration rate had maintained the 1880–1910 average thereafter and if, second, the absolute level of immigration had maintained the 1880–1910 average thereafter? The first sets an upper bound, while the second sets a lower bound on the counterfactual impact. These counterfactuals are reported in the second panel of table 6. Second, the age and sex distribution of the immigrants changed (partly induced by immigration policy), lowering the labor participation rate (and raising the dependency rate) of the interwar immigrants. So, what would have been the impact on 1910–40 labor force growth if, in addition, the immigrant labor participation rate had maintained its 1880–1910 average thereafter? These counterfactuals are reported in the third panel of table 6.

The bottom line is this: The observed decline in the rate of labor force growth 1880–1910 to 1910–40 was 1.15 percentage points, but the no-mass-migration-demise counterfactual decline would have been only between 0.47 (2.29–1.82, third panel) and 0.63 (2.29–1.66, second panel) percentage points. Hence, the demise in mass migration accounted for 45–59 percent of the massive slowdown in U.S. labor force growth around World War I.[5] If the demise in immigration accounted for about half the slowdown in labor supply growth during the interwar years when the world went antiglobal, it must have had an even bigger impact on an unskilled labor supply growth slowdown.

Did the Absence of Immigrants Contribute to the Great Income Leveling in America?

Reverend Thomas Malthus thought that immigration fostered inequality. When appearing before a Parliamentary committee in the 1820s, he argued that Irish immigration into industrial England reduced real wages of the working class and thus raised British poverty rates (Williamson 1986, 694). When the sixth edition of Paul Samuelson's famous *Economics* textbook was published a century and a half later, he joined Malthus with the statement: "After World War I, laws were passed severely limiting immigration. Only a trickle of immigrants has been admitted since then. . . . By keeping labor supply down, immigration policy tends to keep wages high" (Samuelson 1964, cited in Borjas 2003, 2).

This debate has a very old political tradition in the United States that goes back into the late nineteenth century and the appearance of the Dillingham Immigration Commission reports. But the tradition had its origins a half-century earlier, when the first great immigration waves pounded U.S. labor markets:

> The pressures immigration placed on labor markets, particularly in the urban Northeast, produced a remarkable backlash in the 1850s. . . . The popular press took up the anti-immigrant cry with [an editorial stating that] "the enormous influx of foreigners will in the end prove ruinous to American workingmen." (Ferrie 1999, 161–63)

The economics underlying these editorial statements in the 1850s, as well as the comments by Malthus in Britain three decades earlier, has already been laid out in figure 1. To repeat, a glut in the labor supply lowers the wage relative to the returns to capital and rents on land. Since capital and land are held by those at the top of the distribution pyramid, immigration-induced labor supply growth should create more inequality and the demise of immigration should create less, ceteris paribus. If, in addition, immigrants tend to be more unskilled than the native born, then immigration should also raise the premium on skills over the common laborer's wage as skills get relatively scarce, and the demise of immigration should reduce the premium on skills as they get relatively abundant, ceteris paribus. And, by the 1850s, U.S. immigrants had become increasingly unskilled as declining trans-Atlantic transport costs brought overseas emigration within reach of poorer Europeans (for example, the immensely positive selection bias prevailing for 200 years before 1820 had disappeared by 1850; Hatton and Williamson 2004, chapter 3).

Not everyone agrees with this immigration-breeds-inequality position, perhaps because the ceteris-paribus qualifications do not obtain: Many other dynamic forces drove the booming American economy between the 1860s and the 1920s, offering potential offsets to any measured immigrant glut or scarcity. Potential offsets invite debate. For example, Vernon Briggs (1984, 50) thought that the premise of the traditional argument was false, since he believed that immigration was still substantial in the 1920s and productivity advance was very different in rate and bias. Others have argued that immigration generates accumulation responses, forces that would mute the immigration impact. This paper will not resolve the debate, but it will pose the arguments and stress an impressive correlation in the historical time series.

During the mass migrations in the half century before 1913, rich labor-scarce countries with big immigration rates underwent rising inequality, and poor labor-abundant countries with big emigration rates underwent falling inequality (figure 6). During the antiglobal and immigrant-restricted interwar years 1921–38, the correlation disappeared. Indeed, some previously emigrating countries, like Italy, now underwent rising inequality, while some previously immigrating countries, like Australia, Canada, and the United States, underwent falling inequality (figure 7). This is only a correlation, of course: Immigration policy may have been correlated with some omitted variables and the omitted variables may have been doing all the work. Still, at least the correlation does not reject the immigration-breeds-inequality hypothesis.

Now consider figure 8, where we plot the correlation for the United States only, but over 150 years. Figure 8 is taken from a book published some time ago (Williamson and Lindert 1980), and the underlying data have been revised since. Still, the correlation has not been overturned by those revisions; namely, rapid rates of labor force growth in the United States took place during

FIGURE 6

INITIAL LABOR SCARCITY AND DISTRIBUTION TRENDS IN THE GREATER
ATLANTIC ECONOMY, 1870–1913

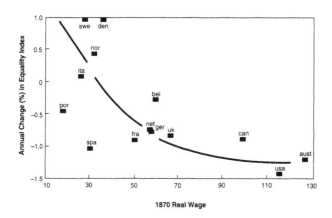

SOURCE: Williamson 1997, figure 6.

FIGURE 7

INITIAL LABOR SCARCITY AND DISTRIBUTION TRENDS IN THE GREATER
ATLANTIC ECONOMY, 1921–1938

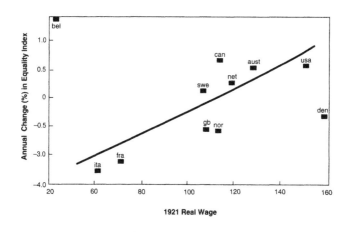

SOURCE: Williamson 1997, figure 7.

FIGURE 8

LABOR SUPPLY AND THE SKILL PREMIUM IN THE UNITED STATES,
1820–1973

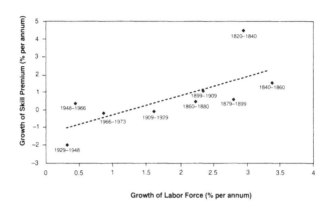

SOURCE: Williamson and Lindert 1980, p. 205.

episodes when earnings inequality was on the rise and the skill premium was increasing, while slow rates of labor force growth took place during episodes when earnings inequality was decreasing and the skill premium was falling. Note the observations 1909–29, 1948–66, and 1966–73 in the lower left-hand quadrant, where the skill premium was stable and the growth rates of the labor force were slow by previous historical standards. Note the observation 1929–48 where labor force growth was especially slow and the collapse in the skill premium spectacular during the "great egalitarian leveling" in America. And note those five pre–World War I observations in the upper right-hand quadrant, where the skill premium was rising and the growth rates in the labor force were fast. Correlation is not causation, but figure 8 is certainly consistent with the immigration-breeds-inequality hypothesis.

The twentieth century evidence on the evolution of U.S. inequality has improved over the past decade or so, thanks to the authors cited in figure 9, and it confirms a great egalitarian leveling in

FIGURE 9
AMERICAN INEQUALITY TRENDS, 1890–1965

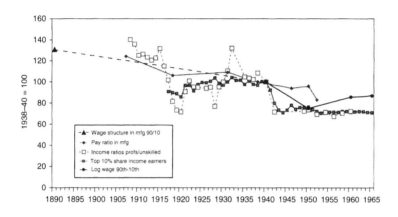

SOURCES AND NOTES: Wage structure in mfg 90/10 = wage ratios, male production workers, top 10 percent relative to bottom 10 percent (Goldin and Katz forthcoming, table 2.1);
income ratios, profs/unskilled = ratio of earnings of college full professors to low-skilled
workers (Goldin and Katz forthcoming, table 2.3); log wage 90th–10th = wage dispersion
of white men, log weekly wages 90th–10th percentiles (Goldin and Margo 1992, table 1);
pay ratio in mfg = pay ratios, skilled to unskilled workers in urban manufacturing (Goldin
and Margo 1992, table VII); top 10 percent share income earners = income share of the
top 10 percent of earners (Piketty and Saez 2003, table II).

American incomes between the first and second thirds of the century. The ratio of wages among the top to the bottom 10 percent in
manufacturing fell by almost a third between 1890 and 1940, a
period of labor force slowdown as we have seen, half of which we
attribute to the demise of mass migration. Pay ratios of skilled to
unskilled workers fell by two-thirds between 1907 and 1952. The
ratio of college professors' incomes to that of unskilled workers was
cut in half between 1908 and 1960. Weekly wage dispersion measures among white men fell by more than a quarter between 1940
and 1965, as did the share of the top 10 percent of income earners.

Among the authors contributing to the evidence in figure 9,
Claudia Goldin and Lawrence Katz have made the greatest effort to
explain the great leveling (Goldin and Margo 1992; Goldin and

Katz 1998, 1999a, 1999b, forthcoming), and the relative demand and supply of skills is central to their story:

> [The] long-run change in the distribution of earnings is shaped by a race between the demand for skill, driven largely by industrial shifts and technological advances, and the supply of skill, altered by changes in educational investments, demographics and immigration. (Goldin and Katz forthcoming, 68)

While Goldin and Katz are cautious, they appear to favor an exogenous and revolutionary change in the supply of secondary and tertiary schooling[6] that must have overwhelmed the skill-using bias that has characterized modern technological progress since the second industrial revolution began a century ago. Such schooling forces would, of course, help erase the skill premium, compress the wage structure, and level incomes. But what about exogenous and revolutionary changes in unskilled labor supplies associated in part with the demise of mass migration? These exogenous policy-induced immigration forces would reinforce the exogenous policy-induced schooling forces: As the growth of the unskilled labor force slowed down and that of skilled labor speeded up, unskilled labor would have gotten scarcer relative to skilled labor. So, is the recent schooling-oriented literature on twentieth century American inequality only half right?

A good illustration of how policy-induced immigration forces created greater unskilled labor scarcity and lower inequality in the United States is not hard to find, and it involves disadvantaged black Americans. Did European immigrants crowd out southern blacks from northern jobs that offered much better earnings and living standards than sharecropping in the South? This is a very old question that was, until recently, illustrated only by compelling correlations. More than thirty years ago, Brinley Thomas (1972, chapter 18, 130–34) noted the striking inverse rhythm between southern black emigration and European immigration to northern cities. The problem left unanswered by the correlations, however, was causation, but William Collins (1997) unraveled the issues and supplied the answers. While only about a half million southern blacks left for the urban North in the four decades before 1910, *seven times* that—about 3.5 million—left in the four decades after 1910. By 1950, one-fifth of all the blacks born in the South now lived in the North.[7] Not only did those who moved improve their economic lives, but those that stayed gained too, since the wage gap between North and South declined sharply as the Great Black Migration better integrated what had been southern labor markets segmented from the rest (Wright 1986). Collins concludes that the mass migrations from Europe did indeed crowd out southern blacks from better jobs in the urban North, and symmetrically, the demise of the mass migrations crowded them in. A very large share of the Great Black Migration can be explained by the disappearance of new European immigrants in northern U.S. cities after 1914.

Since the Great Black Migration greatly improved the relative income position of blacks between 1910 and 1950, it helps account for the great leveling of incomes in the middle third of the twentieth century and offers one important channel through which exogenous changes in European mass migration contributed to the leveling. Historical symmetry also suggests that poorly educated American blacks must have found that increasing immigrant competition after 1970 held back their economic progress.

Explaining Immigration Policy before the 1930s: Political Debate and Backlash

New World doors to immigrants gradually closed after the 1880s. The doors did not suddenly slam shut on American immigrants when the United States Congress overrode President Wilson's veto of the immigrant literacy act in February 1917 or when it passed the Emergency Quota Act of May 1921, since there was plenty of precedent and warning. Over the half-century prior to the literacy act, the United States had been imposing restrictions on what had been free immigration (for example, contract labor laws, Chinese exclusion acts, excludable classes, head taxes, and so on). And the United States was hardly alone. Argentina, Australia, Brazil, and Canada enacted similar measures, although the timing was sometimes different and the policies often took the form of an enormous drop in, or even disappearance of, large immigrant subsidies rather than of outright exclusion. Contrary to the conventional wisdom, therefore, there was not simply one big regime switch around World War I from free (and often subsidized) immigration to quotas but rather an evolution toward a more restrictive immigration policy in the high-wage New World. Attitudes changed slowly and over a number of decades; they did not change all at once.

What explains this evolution in immigration policy? Increasing racism, xenophobia, and widening ethnicity gaps between previous and current immigrants have always been popular candidates. But political economy candidates turn out to be more promising: more immigrants, lower-quality immigrants, the threat of even lower-quality immigrants, crowded-out native unskilled workers, rising inequality, greater awareness of that inequality by the powerful (informed by activist reformers), and greater voting power in the hands of those hurt most, the working poor.

The two central questions for any political economy model of immigration policy are these: First, who gains and who loses? Second, who decides the policy? Let us focus briefly on the second question and who had the vote. A lively literature has emerged recently that explores the rise of suffrage in Europe (Acemoglu and Robinson 2000) and the Americas (Engerman, Haber, and Sokoloff 2000; Sokoloff and Engerman 2000), and it should be helpful in identifying when and where anti-immigration policy emerges in the New World. In 1850, 12.9 percent of the U.S. population voted. If this figure seems small, consider that it almost doubles in size when restricted to males (25.3 percent), doubles again when restricted to male adults (52.3 percent), and increases still further when restricted to white adult men (60.9 percent). In any case, there was no wealth or literacy requirement in the United States in 1850 and no other country had a higher political participation (as a share in total population): The figures were 1.8 percent for Argentina in 1896, Brazil 2.2 percent in 1894, Canada 7.7 percent in 1867, Chile 1.6 percent in 1869, Ecuador 2.8 percent in 1888, and Britain 3.5 percent in 1832 (Sokoloff and Engerman 2000, 225–26; Engerman and Sokoloff 2003, 43). Only after Britain's 1867 act did the vote reach down far enough so that the British "working-class voters became the majority in all urban constituencies," and only after 1870 did "all adult males over the age of 25" have the vote in Germany (Acemoglu and Robinson 2000, 1184).

In short, by 1860 and the end of two decades of very high American immigration rates, the (free, white) workingman had the vote in the United States. Therefore, he had an important voice in the choice of immigration policy. While the rest of the English-speaking overseas immigrant regions were not far behind in giving voting power to their workers, most of Latin America was. But since the United States was the world leader in setting immigration policy and since—as we shall see—the other high-wage immigrant countries followed the leader, it could be said that the American workingman set the policy for all overseas immigrant areas.

The empirical literature on the determinants of immigration policy for the years between 1860 and 1930 is very new, but the main outlines are beginning to emerge (Timmer and Williamson 1998; O'Rourke and Williamson 1999, chapter 10). The most consistent effect is that immigration policy was slow to change. This was especially true of Brazil and the United States: In the latter case, the result is driven by the 1895–1916 period, which included two decades of public scrutiny and congressional debate, ending in the 1917 Immigration Act and the quotas that followed; and in the former case, the result is driven by the 1890–1920 period, when heavily subsidized immigration, financed by fat export earnings generated by high coffee prices, was replaced by restriction and no subsidies when plunging coffee prices generated lean export earnings. It is worth noting that, where historical persistence was strongest, the switch in policy, from open to closed, was biggest. Big immigration policy changes typically required long periods of debate, and the longer the debate, the bigger the change.

Measures of macroeconomic conditions, like unemployment rates, predictably, are of little help in accounting for long-run policy changes. However, the *timing* of the introduction of such policies was powerfully influenced by short-run macroeconomic conditions, often serving as the triggering mechanism.

Labor market conditions had a consistent influence on immigration policy, and they did so both through the absolute and relative income performance of unskilled workers. Real wage growth mattered most in the United States, nominal wage growth mattered most in Australia, while real wage levels mattered most in Brazil. In all cases, poor wage performance was associated with more restrictive policy. However, the most consistently significant explanatory variable is the ratio of the wage of unskilled workers to per-capita income or of income near the bottom of the distribution to income in the middle. Rising inequality was associated with increasingly restrictive immigration policy. As we have seen, new immigrants tended to cluster at the bottom of the income distribution, a fact increasingly true as positive selection diminished over the century. Regardless of what else is included in the regression equation, this measure of labor's relative economic position stands up as an important influence on policy. Rising relative labor scarcity encouraged more open immigration policies; declining relative labor scarcity encouraged more restrictive immigration policies.

The evidence just summarized speaks to the *indirect* impact of immigration on policy by looking at absolute and relative wage performance in labor markets. What about the *direct* impact of immigration on policy? Perhaps the size and character of the current and expected future immigrant flow precipitated policy change, the latter serving to anticipate the labor market impact. Two variables might measure these direct immigration effects. First, one might use a proxy for the quality of the immigrants, here the real wage of unskilled urban workers in the source countries. Second, one might measure immigrant quantity by the foreign-born population share. Low and falling immigrant quality tended to precipitate immigration restrictions in Australia, Canada, and the United States, even after controlling for other forces: Policy in these countries anticipated the impact of rising numbers of low-quality immigrants on wages for the unskilled and moved to exclude them. In addition, Argentina seems to have looked to the north across the Rio de la Plata to watch labor market events in Brazil, acting as if they knew that those events would divert immigrants to or from Argentina's borders. Thus, rising relative and absolute wages in Brazil tended to produce a more open policy in Argentina.

The difference in ethnic composition between the current immigration flow and the foreign population stock seems to have had little bearing on policy. This is not the relationship that the popular literature favors: According to that view, a rising gap between the ethnic origins of previous immigrants, who had become residents and probably voting citizens, and that of current immigrants would erode commitments to free immigration. We should be quick to add that we are speaking almost entirely about immigrants of *European* ethnic origin. The United States and other high-wage countries had already excluded most Asians, and free Africans rarely applied for admission into the historically slave-based New World.

To what extent was a change in a country's policy in part a reaction to policy changes abroad? As expected, the United States was never responsive to competitors' policies, presumably because it was too big and an immigration policy leader. For most of the other countries, policy abroad mattered a great deal. For Argentina, the combined impact of Australian, Canadian, and Brazilian policy mattered; more restrictive policy abroad induced more restrictive policy at home. Brazil tended to mimic the policies followed by the United States. Australia tended to favor open immigration policies when the United Kingdom offered more generous subsidies to its emigrants and, to some extent, when Canada adopted more open policies.

To summarize, while the *size* of the immigrant flow did not seem to have any consistent impact on New World policy up to 1930, its *low and declining quality* certainly did, provoking restriction. Racism and xenophobia do not seem to have been at work in driving the evolution of policy (which is not, of course, to deny that they existed). Rather, immigrant quality, labor market conditions, and policies abroad—especially those set by the economic leaders, Britain and the United States—mattered most for policy. New World countries acted in a way that revealed an effort to defend the economic interests of their scarce factor, unskilled labor.

Summing Up

Over the long haul, the high-wage immigrant countries tried to protect the economic position of their scarce factor, unskilled workers. Labor became relatively more abundant when immigrants poured in, and governments sought to stop any absolute decline in the wages of the native unskilled workers with whom the immigrants competed, often even in their wages relative to the income of those in the middle of the distribution. The greater the perceived threat to these wages from more immigrants, from lower-quality immigrants, or from both, the more restrictive the policy became. And perception is what mattered.

Immigration policy seems to have been influenced indirectly by conditions in the labor market, and directly by immigration forces that, if left to run their course, would have had their impact on labor market conditions. Yet, the switch to more restrictive policies was less a result of rising immigrant flows and foreign-born stocks and more the result of falling immigrant quality. Furthermore, very often immigration policy at home was driven by immigration policy abroad, a correlation that suggests that countries tended to anticipate the likely impact of policies abroad on labor markets at home. Finally, the United States was a clear policy leader, showing no evidence of responding to policies adopted elsewhere; but the remaining immigrant-receiving countries were very sensitive to the leader's policies and the policies of their competitors.

History offers strong support for the proposition that relatively poor labor market conditions and rising inequality played an important role in precipitating the immigration backlash. New

World governments acted to reduce inequality and defend the economic position of unskilled labor and therefore moved to insulate them by restricting immigration. Still, immigration restrictions came late in the first global century, perhaps because unskilled workers did not have a full political voice until late in the century. Economic forces matter for policy, but so do the political institutions with which those forces interact.

Notes

1. The remainder of this paragraph and the next draws on Hatton (2000, 520–25).

2. The recent empirical literature on the determinants of individual attitudes toward immigration cited previously shows that, while negative attitudes toward immigration reflect nationalist sentiment, self-interested economic motivation does indeed matter (Mayda 2003; O'Rourke and Sinnott 2004).

3. A large part of the change in the skill composition was also accommodated by economy-wide skill-biased technical change, thus confirming that technology and factor supplies are always jointly at work.

4. This section on U.S. quotas relies heavily on Gemery (1994, 179–83), who offers the best survey of what is a large literature.

5. The demise in mass migration was not the only force at work, of course, since the crude birth rate in the United States also fell, from about thirty-seven per thousand in the 1880s to about eighteen per thousand in the 1930s.

6. Goldin and Katz treat the schooling supply response as exogenous, but surely the relative scarcity of skilled labor and the high returns to schooling urged governments to invest in education, the Midwest leading the way. And where else would the returns be higher than in the agricultural Midwest, where rural/urban wage gaps were so big (Hatton and Williamson 1991, 1992)?

7. Only a little more than 4 percent of the southern-born blacks lived outside the South at the turn of the century (Collins 1997, 607), or only a fifth of the 1950 figure.

References

Addison, T., and C. Worswick. 2002. The Impact of Immigration on the Earnings of Natives: Evidence from Australian Micro Data. *Economic Record* 78:68–78.

Altonji, J. G., and D. Card. 1991. The Effect of Immigration on the Labor Market Outcomes of Less-Skilled Natives. In *Immigration, Trade and the Labor Market*, ed. J. M. Abowd and R. B. Freeman. Chicago: University of Chicago Press.

Angrist, J. D., and A. D. Kugler. 2003. Protective or Counter Productive: Labor Market Institutions and the Effect of Immigration on UK Natives. *Economic Journal* 113:302–31.

Antecol, H., D. A. Cobb-Clark, and S. K. Trejo. 2003. Immigration Policy and the Skills of Immigrants to Australia, Canada and the United States. *Journal of Human Resources* 38:192–218.

Baker, M., and D. Benjamin. 1994. The Performance of Immigrants in the Canadian Labor Market. *Journal of Labor Economics* 12:455–71.

Bernard, W. S. 1982. A History of U.S. Immigration Policy. In *Immigration*, ed. R. A. Easterlin, D. Ward, W. S. Bernard, and R. Ueda. Cambridge, Mass.: Harvard University Press.

Borjas, G. J. 1987. Self Selection and the Earnings of Immigrants. *American Economic Review* 77:531–53.

———. 1993. Immigration Policy, National Origin, and Immigrant Skills: A Comparison of Canada and the United States. In *Small Differences That Matter: Labor Markets and Income Maintenance in Canada and the United States*, ed. D. Card and R. B. Freeman. Chicago: University of Chicago Press.

———. 1994. The Economics of Immigration. *Journal of Economic Literature* 32 (December): 1667–1717.

———. 1999. The Economic Analysis of Immigration. In *Handbook of Labor Economics*, ed. O. Ashenfelter and D. Card, vol. 3A. New York: North-Holland.

————. 2003. The Labor Demand Curve Is Downward Sloping: Reexamining the Impact of Immigration on the Labor Market. NBER Working Paper 9755. Cambridge, Mass.: National Bureau of Economic Research (June).

Borjas, G. J., R. B. Freeman, and L. F. Katz. 1997. How Much Do Immigration and Trade Affect Labor Market Outcomes? *Brookings Papers on Economic Activity* 1:1–90.

Briggs, V. M. 1984. *Immigration Policy and the American Labor Force.* Baltimore: Johns Hopkins University Press.

Card, D. 1990. The Impact of the Mariel Boatlift on the Miami Labor Market. *Industrial and Labor Relations Review* 43:247–57.

————. 2001. Immigrant Inflows, Native Outflows, and the Local Labor Market Impacts of Higher Immigration. *Journal of Labor Economics* 19:22–64.

Chiquiar, D., and G. H. Hanson. 2002. International Migration, Self-Selection, and the Distribution of Wages: Evidence from Mexico and the United States. NBER Working Paper 9242. Cambridge, Mass.: National Bureau of Economic Research (September).

Clark, X., T. J. Hatton, and J. G. Williamson. 2002. Where Do US Immigrants Come From? Policy and Sending Country Fundamentals. NBER Working Paper 8998. Cambridge, Mass.: National Bureau of Economic Research (June).

Cohen, S., and C.-T. Hsieh. 2000. Macroeconomic and Labor Market Impact of Russian Immigration in Israel. Unpublished paper. Tel Aviv University.

Collins, W. J. 1997. When the Tide Turned: Immigration and the Delay of the Great Migration. *Journal of Economic History* 57 (September): 607–32.

De New, J. P., and K. F. Zimmermann. 1994. Native Wage Impacts of Foreign Labor: A Random Effects Panel Analysis. *Journal of Population Economics* 7:177–92.

Dustmann, C., F. Fabbri, I. Preston, and J. Wadsworth. 2002. The Local Labour Market Effects of Immigration in the UK. UK Home Office Online Report 06/03.

Easterlin, R. A. 1968. *Population, Labor Force and Long Swings in Economic Growth.* New York: National Bureau of Economic Research.

————. 1981. Why Isn't the Whole World Developed? *Journal of Economic History* 41:1–19.

Eckstein, Z., and Y. Weiss. 2003. On the Wage Growth of Immigrants: Israel, 1990–2000. IZA Discussion Paper 710. Bonn: IZA.

Engerman, S. L., S. Haber, and K. L. Sokoloff. 2000. Inequality, Institutions, and Differential Paths of Growth among New World Economies. In *Institutions, Contracts, and Organizations,* ed. C. Menard. Cheltenham, UK: Elgar.

Engerman, S. L., and K. L. Sokoloff. 2003. Institutional and Non-Institutional Explanations of Economic Differences. NBER Working Paper 9989. Cambridge, Mass.: National Bureau of Economic Research (September).

Ferenczi, I., and W. F. Willcox. 1929. *International Migrations,* vol. I. New York: National Bureau of Economic Research.

Ferrie, J. P. 1999. *Yankeys Now: Immigrants in the Antebellum United States, 1840–1860.* New York: Oxford University Press.

Filer, R. K. 1992. The Effect of Immigrant Arrivals on Migratory Patterns of Native Workers. In *Immigration and the Workforce: Economic Consequences for the United States and Source Areas,* ed. G. J. Borjas and R. B. Freeman. Chicago: University of Chicago Press.

Friedberg, R. M. 2001. The Impact of Mass Migration on the Israeli Labor Market. *Quarterly Journal of Economics* 4:1373–1408.

Friedberg, R. M., and J. Hunt. 1995. The Impact of Immigrants on Host-Country Wages, Employment and Growth. *Journal of Economic Perspectives* 9:23–44.

Gemery, H. A. 1994. Immigrants and Emigrants: International Migration and the US Labor Market in the Great Depression. In *Migration and the International Labor Market, 1850–1939,* ed. T. J. Hatton and J. G. Williamson. London: Routledge.

Goldin, C., and L. F. Katz. 1998. The Origins of Technology-Skill Complementarity. *Quarterly Journal of Economics* 113 (June): 693–732.

———. 1999a. The Returns to Skill in the United States across the Twentieth Century. NBER Working Paper 7126. Cambridge, Mass.: National Bureau of Economic Research (May).

———. 1999b. Egalitarianism and the Returns to Education during the Great Transformation of American Education. *Journal of Political Economy* 107:65–94.

———. Forthcoming. Decreasing (and Then Increasing) Inequality in America: A Tale of Two Half Centuries. In *The Causes and Consequences of Increasing Inequality.* Chicago: University of Chicago Press.

Goldin, C., and R. A. Margo. 1992. The Great Compression: The Wage Structure in the United States at Mid-Century. *Quarterly Journal of Economics* 107:1–34.

Hammermesh, D. 1993. *Labor Demand.* Princeton, N.J.: Princeton University Press.

Hanson, G. H., and M. J. Slaughter. 2002. Labor-Market Adjustment in Open Economies: Evidence from US States. *Journal of International Economics* 57 (June): 3–29.

Hatton, T. J. 2000. How Much Did Immigrant "Quality" Decline in Late Nineteenth Century America? *Journal of Population Economics* 13:509–25.

Hatton, T. J., and M. Tani. 2003. Immigration and Inter-Regional Mobility in the UK, 1982–2000. CEPR Discussion Paper 4061. London: Centre for Economic Policy Research.

Hatton, T. J., and J. G. Williamson. 1991. Wage Gaps between Farm and City: Michigan in the 1890s. *Explorations in Economic History* 28 (October): 381–408.

———. 1992. What Explains Wage Gaps between Farm and City? Exploring the Todaro Model with American Evidence, 1890–1941. *Economic Development and Cultural Change* 40 (January): 267–94.

———. 1998. *The Age of Mass Migration: An Economic Analysis.* New York: Oxford University Press.

———. Forthcoming. *World Mass Migration: Two Centuries of Policy and Performance.*

Hendricks, L. 2002. How Important Is Human Capital for Development? Evidence from Immigrant Earnings. *American Economic Review* 92:198–219.

Hunt, J. 1992. The Impact of the 1962 Repatriates from Algeria on the French Labor Market. *Industrial and Labor Relations Review* 45:556–72.

Kirk, D. 1946. *Europe's Population in the Interwar Years.* Princeton, N.J.: Princeton University Press for the League of Nations.

Kuznets, S., and E. Rubin. 1954. *Immigration and the Foreign-Born.* New York: National Bureau of Economic Research.

Lalonde, R. J., and R. H. Topel. 1991. Labor Market Adjustments to Increased Immigration. In *Immigration, Trade and the Labor Market,* ed. J. M. Abowd and R. B. Freeman. Chicago: University of Chicago Press.

Lindert, P. H. 2003. *Growing Public: Social Spending and Economic Growth since the Eighteenth Century.* Cambridge: Cambridge University Press.

Maddison, A. 1991. *Dynamic Forces in Capitalist Development: A Long-Run Comparative View.* Oxford: Oxford University Press.

Mayda, A. M. 2003. Who Is Against Immigration? A Cross-Country Investigation of Individual Attitudes towards Immigrants. Mimeo, Harvard University (January).

O'Rourke, K. H., and R. Sinnott. 2004. The Determinants of Individual Attitudes towards Immigration. Mimeo. Trinity College Dublin (January).

O'Rourke, K. H., and J. G. Williamson. 1999. *Globalization and History: The Evolution of a Nineteenth-Century Atlantic Economy.* Cambridge, Mass.: MIT Press.

Piketty, T., and E. Saez. 2003. Income Inequality in the United States, 1913–1998. *Quarterly Journal of Economics* 118 (February): 1–39.

Pischke, J.-S., and J. Velling. 1997. Employment Effects of Immigration to Germany: An Analysis Based on Local Labor Markets. *Review of Economics and Statistics* 79:594–604.

Sokoloff, K. L., and S. L. Engerman. 2000. Institutions, Factor Endowments, and Paths of Development in the New World. *Journal of Economic Perspectives* 14 (Summer): 217–32.

Taylor, A. M., and J. G. Williamson. 1997. Convergence in the Age of Mass Migration. *European Review of Economic History* 1:27–63.

Thomas, B. 1972. *Migration and Urban Development.* London: Methuen.

Timmer, A., and J. G. Williamson. 1998. Immigration Policy Prior to the Thirties: Labor Markets, Policy Interaction, and Globalization Backlash. *Population and Development Review* 24 (December): 739–71.

Williamson, J. G. 1982. Immigrant-Inequality Trade-Offs in the Promised Land: American Growth, Distribution and Immigration Prior to the Quotas. In *The Gateway: U.S. Immigration Issues and Policies*, ed. B. Chiswick. Washington, D.C.: AEA Press.

———. 1986. The Impact of the Irish on British Labor Markets during the Industrial Revolution. *Journal of Economic History* 56 (September): 693–720.

———. 1997. Globalization and Inequality, Past and Present. *World Bank Research Observer* 12 (August): 117–35.

Williamson, J. G., and P. H. Lindert. 1980. *American Inequality: A Macroeconomic History.* New York: Academic Press.

Wright, G. 1986. *Old South, New South.* New York: Basic Books.

Ziliboth, F., and J. Robinson. 2000. Why Did the West Extend the Franchise? Democracy, Inequality, and Growth in Historical Perspective. *Quarterly Journal of Economics* 115 (November): 1167–99.

About the Author

Jeffrey G. Williamson is the Laird Bell Professor of Economics at Harvard University, where he is a faculty fellow at the Center for International Development and a faculty associate at the Weatherhead Center for International Affairs. He is also a research associate at the National Bureau of Economic Research. Professor Williamson received his PhD from Stanford University and taught at the University of Wisconsin for twenty years before joining the Harvard faculty in 1983.

The author of more than twenty books and almost two hundred scholarly articles in economic history, international economics, and economic development, Professor Williamson has served as president of the Economic History Association, chairman of the Economics Department at Harvard, and master of Mather House at Harvard. His most recent books include *Growth, Inequality, and Globalization* (Mattioli Lectures: Cambridge, 1998, with P. Aghion), *Globalization and History* (MIT, 1999, with K. O'Rourke), and *Globalization in Historical Perspective* (Chicago and NBER, 2002, with M. Bordo and A. M. Taylor). This AEI Wendt Lecture draws extensively on a forthcoming book written with Timothy Hatton, entitled *World Mass Migration: Two Centuries of Policy and Performance*. Professor Williamson is currently working on a forthcoming book entitled *Globalization and the Poor Periphery in the Pre-Modern Era*.